BLINKY
BLINKY
BLINKY
BLINKY
BLINKY

DOG

£5.99

D0548453

SNEAKER'S
SLY SNEAKS

Later —

AH, THIS IS NICE.

Then —

COME ON, DAD — I WANT TO GO ON THAT.

ANYTHING FOR A QUIET LIFE.

THE BIG WHEEL

So —

WHAT'S THE BUCKET FOR? IS IT IN CASE YOU GET SICK?

NOT QUITE.

I'M GOING TO HAVE BUCKETS OF FUN!

OH, NO!

GROWING PAYNES

Soon after —

Smasher

Shortly —

LUCKILY FOR ME THERE WAS A BUNCH OF BANANAS IN THAT BIN.

NOW TO CATCH BLIGHT AND HIS PAL DOCTOR GLOOM.

NOT SO FAST, BLIGHTY. YOUR NAUGHTY GAME IS OVER.

YOU CAN LAUGH — I'VE STILL CAUGHT YOU.

YEAH! HO! HO!

TOOT! TOOT!

ULP! THAT SOUNDS CLOSE.

HUNTERS FROM THE SKIES

BIRDS OF PREY SEEN IN BRITAIN

LONG-EARED. OWL

BARN OWL

HOBBY

KITE

MERLIN

SPARROW-HAWK

COMMON BUZZARD

MARSH HARRIER

GOLDEN EAGLE

This is the largest of all British birds of prey. Male golden eagles have a wing-span of up to 7 feet. The wing-span of the female is about a foot more.

KESTREL

TAWNY OWL

LITTLE OWL

PEREGRINE FALCON

OSPREY or FISHING-HAWK

MONTAGU'S HARRIER

HONEY BUZZARD

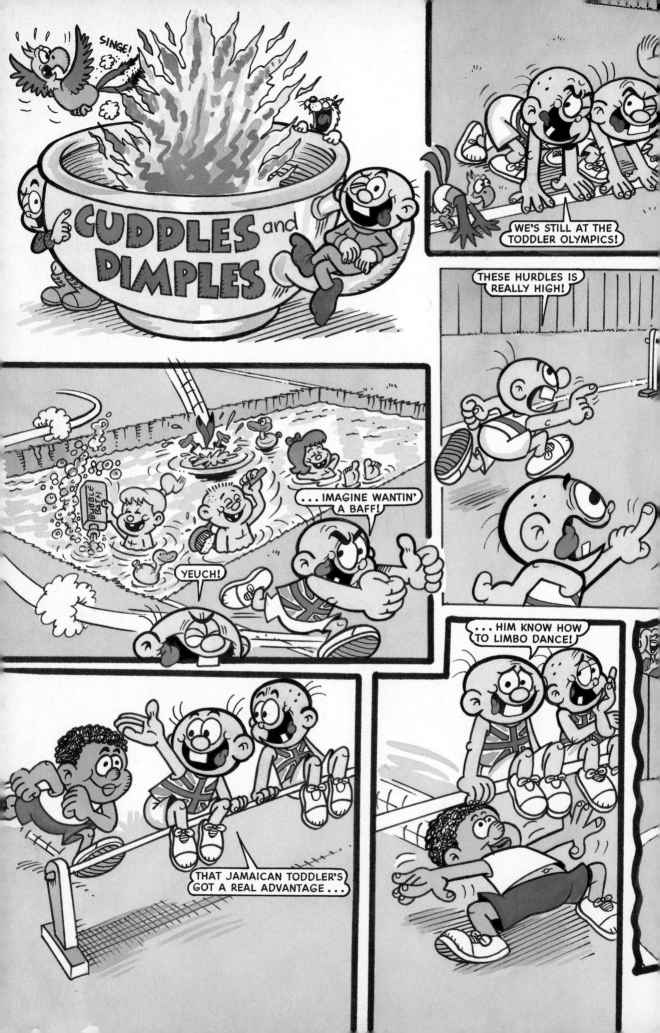

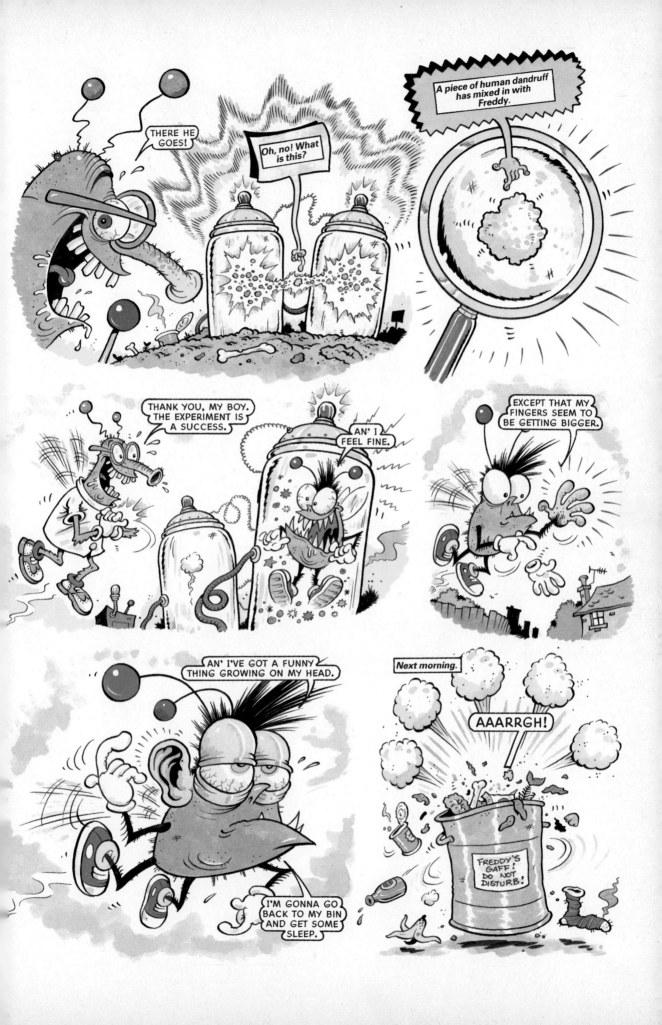

Kalamity Kitchens

At Cholesterol High...

WHAT'S FOR DINNER TODAY, CARROT?

STEW!

IT'S SO FRESH I CAN'T CATCH IT!

HOOTS!

OOPS!

MAYBE NOT! A RIGHT BUNCH OF PORKERS IN THE THIRD FORM.

BACKING OFF.

I'VE MADE SOMETHING, SAUSAGE.

Carrot. Sausage. Crackers. Stew.

BAH! IT'S YOU, STEW! GET OUT OF IT!

SAYS FRESH HAGGIS FOR LUNCH TODAY.

EVERYBODY LOVES A GOOD FRY-UP.

WHEN IN DOUBT, GIVE 'EM BACON BUTTIES, THAT'S WHAT I SAY.

DINING HALL.

H, DEAR. HATE TO INK WHAT CKERS HAS MADE.

WOW! CHIPS! WELL DONE, CRACKERS. SERVE THEM UP.

SURE . . .

. . . GREAT FOR LAYING PATHS.

AS YOU CAN SEE THE PUPILS AROUND HERE LOVE OUR MAD MENU. HA! HA!

MOLLY

SPORE

Helsinki — in living memory winter has always brought long, cold, dark nights . . .

. . . but early in the next century that is changed.

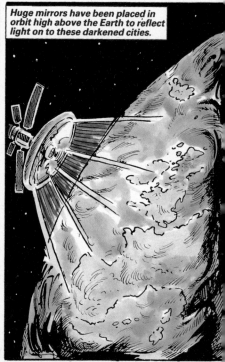

Huge mirrors have been placed in orbit high above the Earth to reflect light on to these darkened cities.

And it is one of these mirrors which shows the first evidence of the coming danger . . .

. . . a meteorite hurtles into Earth's atmosphere.

Oxford Observatory —

LOOK, DAD — A SHOOTING STAR.

IT'S THAT METEOR WE'VE BEEN TRACKING, JENNI. IT'S COMING DOWN.

CAN WE GO, DAD? IT ONLY HIT A FEW MILES AWAY.

TOMORROW MORNING. WE WON'T BE ABLE TO SEE ANYTHING INTERESTING TONIGHT.

Jenni's Dad knew what he was talking about. He should have been right.

Should have been — but he wasn't.

Next morning —

I'VE NEVER SEEN A REAL METEOR BEFORE.

WYV 611

ME NEITHER. I THINK I'M MORE EXCITED THAN YOU.

But —

THIS CAN'T BE RIGHT. IT CAN'T . . .

THERE SHOULDN'T BE ANY PLANT-LIFE LEFT ALIVE AFTER THE EXPLOSION.

IT'S GROWING OUT OF THE METEOR.

AMAZING — AN ALIEN PLANT LIFE-FORM.

IT'LL NEVER SURVIVE THOSE BOMBS. THEY'RE THE MOST POWERFUL OUR PLANES CARRY.

But—

CONTROL, IT'S ATTACKING US!

RETREAT! EVERYBODY PULL BACK.

WE CAN'T STOP IT. EVEN OUR MOST ADVANCED BOMBS ARE HAVING NO EFFECT.

WE MUST BE ABLE TO DO SOMETHING — IT'S ONLY A PLANT.

TRY BUNGING IT IN A DARK CUPBOARD AND NOT WATERING IT FOR A WHILE.

THAT'S IT! YOU'RE BRILLIANT, JENNI!

I AM?

WHATEVER YOU'RE PLANNING, MAKE IT QUICK. THE PLANT HAS CLOSED US IN.

Jenni had given her Dad an idea — plants need light . . .

. . . and he had a plan to block out the sun . . .

. . . by moving the mirrors in space so that they were between the Sun and Earth.

THE PLANT IS INACTIVE IN THE DARK SO KEEP THE MIRRORS IN PLACE.

THIS ROBBERY.

WE'RE JUST TAKIN' THE CASH INTO POLICE CUSTODY.

YOU ROTTERS!

TALKIN' OF ROTTERS, WHO MADE THAT SMELL?

IT'S ONLY ME, BOYS. YOUR FAVOURITE PIN-UP GIRL.

SKUNK WOMAN. PH-EW!

WHEN I HEARD YOU WERE IN CHARGE OF THE POLICE FORCE I SMELT MONEY.

Meanwhile, Little Eric is at home —

SNIFF! SO NOBODY WANTS BANANAMAN ANY MORE. I WON'T LET IT BOTHER ME.

NOT WANTED ANYMORE

GROAN! WHAT'S THIS? CHOCOLATE?

FROM THAT I DEDUCE THAT THE VILLAIN AND THE CAKE ARE IN MY TREE-HOUSE AND THE PILFERER IS...

...MY SISTER, MARSHA!

ULP! NABBED!

YOU'RE IN DEEP TROUBLE, SIS. GOT ANYTHING TO SAY BEFORE I TAKE YOU IN?

COO! CAKE!

BEAUTIFUL BIRDS OF BRITAIN

ROBIN

BLUE TIT

JAY

LINNET

MAGPIE

CHAFFINCH

GOLDFINCH

SWALLOW

KINGFISHER

GREY WAGTAIL

PHEASANT

HAWFINCH

HOOPOE

GOLDEN ORIOLE

LAPWING

YELLOW-HAMMER

STARLING

NUTHATCH

GREEN WOODPECKER

RED GROUSE

DOTTEREL

GREAT SPOTTED WOODPECKER

GROWING PAYNES

Soon —

Meanwhile —

SEA BIRDS
SEEN AROUND BRITAIN'S SHORES.

BLACK-GUILLEMOT

REDNECKED-PHALAROPE

OYSTER-CATCHER

PINKFOOTED-GOOSE

SHOVELER

RAZORBILL

GREAT CRESTED-GREBE

GOOSANDER

TEAL

EIDER-DUCK

ROSEATE-TERN

REDBREASTED-MERGANSER

GANNET

PUFFIN

SHAG

SHELDRAKE

BARNACLE-GOOSE

MALLARD

GREAT NORTHERN-DIVER

PINTAIL

GREAT BLACKBACKED-GULL

Kalamity Kitchens

Shallot.

POP!

ERK!

HAGGIS IS JUST BORROWING THEM FOR A LITTLE SWORD DANCE.

HOOTS, MON!

PRANCE!

GRIEF! 'U'RE SED TO AFTER PPING ONS! GOES SOUP.

WHY DON'T WE MAKE 'EM JAM BUTTIES?

JAM

GREAT IDEA! GET SPREADING, TOASTIE.

Toastie.

DEAR. STIE IS N A AM!

BUT NEVER MIND, THE KIDS WILL SOON HAVE IT LICKED!

LICK!

SLURP!

HEE! HEE! HEE! STOP IT! THAT TICKLES.

BEDTIME TALES

with BRADLEY BEDSOCK

LICK! **P SUCK!**

Polar explorer Sebastian Snowshoe huddled in his tent, sucking an ice lolly. Actually, the lolly was a mug of chicken soup with the spoon frozen into it. Sebastian was alone in the dismal Arctic wastes, in the middle of a terrible snowstorm, on a night when the temperature plummeted quicker than an elephant doing a bungee jump.

The rest of the expedition party had left Sebastian the previous week. They had returned to civilisation, frustrated at his inept leadership, the lack of decent slopes to go sledging on and the fact that he didn't allow snowball fights. Sebastian insisted they were bad for morale and started another game of 'I Spy'. "I spy, with my little eye, something beginning with . . . S," he began. "SNOW!" chorused his fed-up chums and left.

LICK!

ICED SOUP

SHIVER

TRIP!

TEA

Sebastian had maintained a stiff upper lip as he watched his former comrades depart. (The icicles on his moustache would have given anyone a stiff upper lip). He turned his back on the laughing, rasping figures and prepared to continue his quest for the famed Santa Claus lost toy store alone.

Was this the abominable snowman of legend? The enormous ape-like beast that has terrified Arctic adventurers down through the ages? Well, whatever it was, it was pretty abominable! A hideous scrunched-up face with deep-set eyes, a long shaggy coat and enormous feet — that was what Sebastian saw as he opened the flap of his tent.

④

Actually, that's not true! Inadvertently, Sebastian had disovered the hidden toy store ⑥ beneath the ice and had caught his neck on a hula-hoop. That's what killed him. The abominable snowman? That was Eskimo Del, who had been trying to rescue the mad explorer. He was wearing large fur boots and a large fur coat with its hood up. He had a fur scarf over his mouth and the growling noises were him singing Eskimo folk songs that suffered badly by being muffled by the scarf.

HULA-HOOPS

SANTA'S HIDDEN TOY STORE

⑧ This story was written by actors and no insane Arctic idiots were harmed during the writing of this tale.